A Child's First Library of Learning

Everyday Life

TIME-LIFE BOOKS • ALEXANDRIA, VIRGINIA

Contents

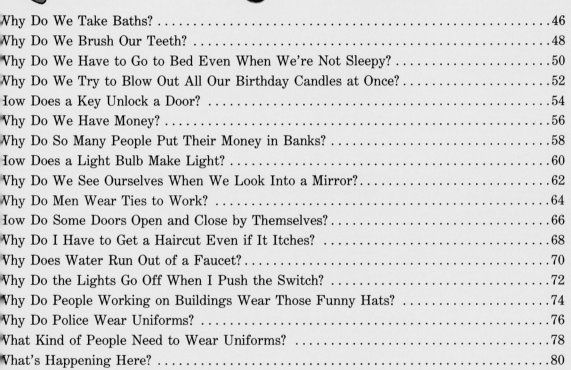

❓ Why Do We Wash Every Morning?

ANSWER Washing our faces in the morning is a good way to wake up. It gets the sleep out of our eyes. It stops us from yawning. It washes away the sweaty stickiness that may have collected while we slept. It makes us feel clean and fresh and ready to face the new day.

Before washing your face

I'm so sleepy I can't open my eyes.

After washing your face

Hey, that's better! I feel wide awake now.

■ The best way to wash your face

Keep your fingers close together. Cup your hands and scoop up some water.

Lean forward and splash the water over your face. Don't spill any!

Wash your face well, then dry it on a towel. Dry your hands well, too.

Your mother and father wash their faces too. Do they do anything else?

Father shaves his beard with a razor.

Sometimes mother puts on makeup.

When we wake up in the morning, our faces look very sleepy. As soon as we wash up, that sleepy morning look goes away.

We get hot and sticky when we're asleep, so washing our faces gets rid of the sweat, too.

● To the Parent

Although washing one's face every morning is second nature to most adults, young children will need to be taught this habit. Explain to them that cool water on the face helps wake you after a comfortable night's sleep. It is a good idea to get a small child into this routine as soon as possible. The little ones find it difficult to scoop water up in their hands, so you will have to supervise them well at first, and though a few damp floors may result they will soon learn how to do it. Teaching by example is very effective. Letting them see how you go about it, and that you make a habit of washing your face properly every morning, will considerably facilitate the learning process.

? Why Do We Dress in the Morning?

ANSWER Look at your pajamas when you put them on. They fit loosely so you can be comfortable in bed. And when you sweat at night they soak up the moisture. That's why you take them off and change into ordinary clothes that are dry and look nice.

■ Suppose you went out in your pajamas...

People would think you were still asleep and laugh at you.

And if you got them dirty, what would you wear at night?

■ Other times when we change our clothes

We have ordinary day clothes, and we have clothes we wear on special occasions, like when we're being taken on a treat. We also have clothes we wear when we're playing games outdoors, or when we're running in races.

▲ **When exercising.** We usually change into our sports clothes so we can move about more easily.

▲ **For sleeping.** Most people usually wear night clothes like pajamas or a nightgown.

Dolly wants to change clothes too, don't you?

▲ **Going somewhere special.** On a treat or visiting relatives we dress in our best clothes.

● **To the Parent**

Small children often find having to change into day clothes a bother, but it is as important as washing their faces for making the start of the new day. Although you will have to help them while they are small, they will soon want to try for themselves. At first mismatched buttons and shirttails out will be the result, but they will learn by experience and be dressing themselves properly in no time at all.

❓ Where Does All Our Food Come From?

ANSWER All sorts of people work very hard to produce the food we eat. Our parents work hard to make money to buy food. They also work hard preparing it. So you can see that much effort goes into the food we eat. That's why it's nice to show your appreciation by saying "Thank you, that was really good," when you finish eating.

> All kinds of different people have worked hard to produce the things we eat.

> Wow! Looks good!

● **To the Parent**

Food is plentiful and varied in most countries, but modern distribution systems have distanced most of us from the producer, so it is easy to take our food for granted. It is important that children appreciate the efforts required to produce and purchase it. Use the food on the table, daily shopping trips and visits to the country to foster a sense of appreciation in them.

◀ Rice is
harvested
by farmers.

▶ Fresh green
vegetables
are now ripe.

◀ Fresh fish
is sold in
a market.

▶ Farmers sell
vegetables
in a market.

Thanks, Mom
and Dad. That
was good!

? Why Must Our Parents Work?

ANSWER Many mothers and fathers leave home every morning to go to work. In return for their hard work they receive money. Your parents use this money to buy the things that your family needs, such as food and clothing.

▼ Some parents have offices. They work there together with many other people.

■ Your parents' work and your life at home

Everything we need to live, such as food, clothing and a place to live, and things we enjoy having, like a nice house, books and toys, all have to be bought with money. Where does that money come from? It's the money your parents bring home from work. They work hard so that your family can have a safe, happy, comfortable and pleasant life.

What Kinds of Work Do Parents Do?

There are many different kinds of jobs that people do. All of these jobs are important to you and to the people in the community where you live.

▲ Farmers work in the fields and tend animals.

▼ A doctor takes care of her patients' health.

▲ Factory workers make the things that we use.

● **To the Parent**

Most adults have some kind of job, and in some families both parents work. Although children realize that their parents leave the house each day it is difficult for them to understand where they go or what they do, and particularly to grasp the concept of money. It is important to explain to the child that everything the family possesses, the food it eats and the things it enjoys, are purchased with money earned by one or both parents. Today work patterns are more varied than ever. Discuss with your child who works in your family. Make sure that your child understands that work done around the house is also important to the family's well-being.

11

What Can We Do To Help Around the House?

ANSWER You are old enough to help around the house, and there are lots of things that you can do. You can help set the table before meals. You can clear the table after everyone has finished eating. You can take out the trash. Ask your parents how you can be most helpful.

■ Other things you can do to help

▲ Help your brother when he goes to the supermarket.

▲ Sweep the sidewalk and help keep the yard clean.

❓ Why Must We Keep Our Home Clean?

ANSWER Because if dust and dirt collect they make a place where germs love to live. And germs can make us ill. That's why a clean, tidy house is always a happy, healthy place to live.

Keeping the World Around Us Clean Is Important Too

As well as keeping our house clean, it's important to keep the world around us clean. That will make it a much nicer place to live in. Everyone can help keep our streets, parks and mountains clean and free from litter. You can help too. Don't scatter litter around. Always put it in a litter bin. You're sure to find one nearby if you look hard enough.

▶ A sad sight! Empty cans littering a mountainside. Let's keep our mountains beautiful.

⊿ Garbage from the house is taken away in refuse trucks.

▲ Litter is cleared off the mountainside.

⊿ Leaves are raked into piles for burning.

 TRY THIS

Things for cleaning

Some things used for cleaning the house are appliances. Others are mops, brooms, buckets and the like. Try looking around your house and see what sort of cleaning tools you can find. You're sure to find some of the things in this picture.

● **To the Parent**

As the amount of refuse generated by our modern society increases, waste disposal becomes a pressing concern of the whole community. Start at home by encouraging your children to help around the house, and let them experience first hand the correlation between cleanliness and good health and gain an appreciation of parents' efforts in this area. Parents serve as role models for a child's developing community consciousness. Teach them to put litter in the receptacles provided, wherever they are.

Why Do We Say Good Morning When We Meet People We Know?

ANSWER Greetings let people know how we feel about them. They show that we like them and respect them, and they help us all get along better with one another. If someone you know greets you, it's friendly and polite to greet them back.

Good morning! Oh my! They didn't even notice me!

Good morning!

MINI-DATA

In a lot of countries greetings are different at different times of the day. When you're out with someone older, listen carefully to how they greet other people.

Greetings change during the day

▲ **Good morning**

▲ **Good afternoon**

▲ **Good evening**

16

Some other greetings that are often used

• To the Parent

It is frequently said that the day begins and ends with a word of greeting. Greetings fulfill the important social function of facilitating our relationships with one another. A child's repertoire of greetings begins with a few simple but basic expressions learned by imitating its parents. These are developed and increased when the child encounters the wider social environment found outside the home, such as that of nursery school or kindergarten. It is recommended that parents encourage their child to make use of these newly acquired expressions in their everyday life at home. The greetings shown on this page are examples of how we might greet people, say goodbye, apologize or express appreciation.

Why Do We Always Walk on the Sidewalk?

ANSWER Sometimes busy roads are filled with cars going in many directions. We stay on the sidewalk to be safe from the traffic. When there is no sidewalk it is all right to walk in the road, but we walk facing traffic. In this way we can see the cars that are coming near us.

Use the Special Path For People on Foot

Some roads have a special path for people on foot, but some do not.

Careful how you go now!

▲ It is safest to cross the street with adults.

▲ Safety patrols help children cross the street.

Why Can't We Cross the Street When the Light Is Red?

ANSWER Because a red light facing us at a pedestrian crossing means "Stop! Danger! Cars moving!" Green means "Traffic stopped. Look both ways! Cross now!"

Whether you are crossing the road at a pedestrian crossing or a place where there are no traffic lights, always look both ways carefully before you cross. "Left, right, left!" when cars drive on the right. "Right, left and right again!" when they drive on the left. Always use a pedestrian bridge or underpass whenever there is one. It's far safer than crossing the road.

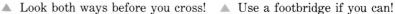

▲ Look both ways before you cross!   ▲ Use a footbridge if you can!

Don't Cross Until
The Light Is Green!

Green!
It's safe!
Cross now!

Green flashing
means danger!
Don't cross!

Red! Stop!
Danger!
Don't cross!

● **To the Parent**

In the busy street scene above, pedestrians are using a system of flags to ensure greater safety while crossing the street. This system is used in some countries. Ask your child to tell you how he knows when it is safe to cross the street where you live. Train your child to use crosswalks and obey red and green traffic signals.

Why Are Pets Not Allowed In Some Apartment Buildings?

(ANSWER) Apartment buildings can be very crowded places. Dogs that are not properly trained can make a lot of noise. Cats can scratch carpets in the hallways. So in some buildings these kinds of pets are not allowed.

If you are lucky enough to have a dog as a pet, make sure it doesn't annoy other people by barking late at night.

▲ Pets make good friends.

I wish he'd be quiet. I can't get to sleep!

■ Imagine what would happen if you had too many pets

▲ Be sure to feed your pets so they stay healthy.

Pets can get into all sorts of mischief if they haven't been trained properly. Don't let this happen to you! Start training your pet gently but firmly from the moment you get it.

Why Can't We Get on the Train As Soon as It Stops?

ANSWER Because there are people on the train waiting to get off. If we tried to get on right away, they wouldn't be able to get off. The people getting off make room in the car for those boarding, so it's smart to stand back and wait for them. And it's more polite, too!

▲ People waiting to get on a train let others off first.

▲ **Elevators.** They are like trains. Stand aside and let others off.

❓ What About Buses? Are They the Same?

Sometimes, if there is only one place for passengers to get on and off. But if there is a place for getting on and a separate place for getting off, we line up and get on one at a time when it is our turn. Where to get on and off the bus may be different in different countries.

● **To the Parent**

Explaining the correct way to use the trains can serve to introduce your child to some basic rules of social behavior. Teach them about waiting their turn. Use actual experiences. Trains and elevators are good for showing them how to behave if there is only one exit door, buses for when there is more than one. But remember that the position of the doors can vary on different buses.

▲ Here they get on at the front and off in the middle.

25

Why Is It Wrong to Play Around And Make Noise on Trains?

ANSWER It can be dangerous. Trains move fast and swing around. If you don't sit or stand still and hold on, you might fall and hurt yourself. And it disturbs other passengers if you play or run around and make noise.

Some Other Places Where You Shouldn't Be Noisy

Libraries, hospitals and those places where other people are quiet are the sort of places where we should all try hard to be quiet and well-behaved.

▲ **A library.** Noise isn't allowed. We come here to read books and we have to be quiet to do that.

▲ **A doctor's office.** Most of the people visiting here do not feel well. It is unkind to disturb them.

● **To the Parent**

Small children have difficulty with conceptual explanations, so it is better to teach them respect for other people's feelings in actual situations. Point out to them that other people on the train are sitting or standing quietly, and explain to them why it is important that they behave in the same manner.

Why Must We Sometimes Eat Foods We Don't Like?

ANSWER Sometimes things you don't like are the things that are best for you. You may not know it, but your parents know that these foods are very nourishing. The parts of food that make us healthy and strong are called nutrients. They are found in foods we don't like as well as in those we like.

Why Do Different Foods Have Different Tastes?

If all the food we ate tasted the same we would soon get bored with it. Yes, even with our favorite food! The dishes we eat taste different because of the variety of ingredients used. That is what makes food tasty and fun to eat. It makes us grow up big and strong too!

Children who eat everything up are strong and healthy!

Sigh! I'm so worn out!

If you eat the wrong foods you will have no energy.

● **To the Parent**

It is all too easy for some children to become picky eaters, and once this is established it can prove a difficult pattern to correct. Yet with a little effort on your part this need not happen. Start early getting your child excited about food. Explain which nutrients are found in which foods and how the body uses them as energy and to build tissue, and how this is connected with being healthy and strong. Making less-favored dishes as palatable as you can also helps. A balanced diet includes all three major food groups: protein, carbohydrates and fats. The body manufactures all of these but not the vitamins essential to good health, which can be supplied only in the food we eat. Here's a brief list of how the body uses these and some of the foods in which they can be found. Proteins and vitamin B build muscle and blood. Poultry, eggs, meat, fish, beans, nuts and dairy products are excellent sources of protein and the mineral salts that build bones and teeth. Carbohydrates provide body energy and are found in grains, vegetables and sugar from fruit. But eating too much sugar, especially refined sugar, is not healthy. Fats, which are found mostly in animal products and in all kinds of oil, and vitamin A, vitamin C, calcium and iodine are essential for strength and maintaining body temperature.

Why Do People Eat With a Fork and Spoon?

ANSWER We eat many kinds of food. Forks and spoons help us pick up these foods without making a mess, and that makes a meal more enjoyable.

■ Sometimes we still eat with our hands

In most cases it is not polite to eat with your hands. But for some foods, like fried chicken, even grown-ups might want to eat with their hands.

■ Chopsticks help too

Not everyone uses forks and spoons. In Asia many foods are cut up before cooking or are things like noodles, so it is easier to eat them with chopsticks.

■ An ordinary table setting

In restaurants or at parties you may find several knives, forks and spoons. As you use the pieces for each course they are removed from the table.

Why Do Some Children Like the Cold?

ANSWER In many countries it gets very cold in winter. But children who are happy and healthy don't mind the cold at all. They just put on a lot of warm clothes and go out and play just the same.

They don't have to stay in even when it's cold. They wrap up well and go out and have fun!

▲ A brisk rubdown with a rough towel will make them toasty warm if they are feeling chilly.

● **To the Parent**

In colder climates healthy children can be found wrapped up and playing outside in all weather. Nourishing food, lots of sleep and plenty of exercise are the best protection to give them against colds and flu. If you live in a colder region, tell them that cold germs hate fresh air and won't follow them outside. Encourage them to get plenty of exercise in the right kind of clothes, with lots of time out in the air.

Why Aren't We Allowed To Play in the Road?

ANSWER Usually when we're playing we forget everything else. If we were playing in the road, we probably wouldn't see the cars coming and might get run over and hurt. We don't play in the road. It's far too dangerous.

Then Where Is It Safe to Play?

There are lots of places where it is safe to play. Parks are good. Playgrounds too. But always tell a grown-up where you will be playing.

▲ Here's a good place to play.

▲ Many parks have playgrounds where children can play.

▲ This street's safe because it's closed to traffic.

● **To the Parent**

Do you know your child's favorite spots to play? Are they safe? Point out all the attractions to be found in parks and playgrounds, and encourage your children to play in those. Simply telling them that they must not play in the road, or anywhere, often enhances the attraction. Make an agreement with them about where they should play. Take their desires into consideration, explain the dangers, set reasonable limits, and make them promise to always tell you where they are going to be. Then you will have safe, happy children who trust you even when you say no.

Why Must We Always Wait Our Turn On the Playground Equipment?

ANSWER Just think for a minute. Take the slide in the playground. Everyone likes the slide, but if we didn't take turns, it wouldn't be fair. Arguments would start, and we wouldn't be able to play happily.

■ **Here's what could happen if we didn't take turns**

▲ It's my turn! I was here first!

▲ I don't care! I'm going first, so there!

It's correct to wait your turn wherever you may be!

▲ You should wait your turn to go on the rides.

▲ You should wait in line at the school cafeteria.

▲ You should wait in line to get on the school bus.

▲ We don't like you! You don't play fair!

● **To the Parent**

Groups naturally establish rules. Children need to understand that their rights and the rights of others are protected if they observe the rules, but that not doing so could result in arguments and dissension, with ostracism from the group a natural adjunct. Use real life situations to demonstrate how you follow the same rules by standing in line when shopping or getting on trains and buses. Teach your child to adhere to the rules of various social situations. Gently explain how flouting the rules, wanting preferential treatment or his own way can lead to ostracism and the feeling of loneliness by which, invariably, this is accompanied.

Why Can't We Play Outside After It Gets Dark?

ANSWER Because we can't see things so clearly in the dark and could easily trip over something, or get hit by a ball that someone throws to us. Playing outside after dark can be dangerous, so to keep safe and happy, we go home before it gets dark.

■ The sun sets at different times

Because days are longer in summer and shorter in winter, sunset is later in summer than in winter. Even though we are having fun playing, we should remember to go home before it starts to get dark.

▲ It's 6 o'clock and still light on this sunny day.

▲ It's 4 o'clock, but it's winter in this northern country, so it is already starting to get dark.

● **To the Parent**

Children can get so absorbed in their activities that they become oblivious to everything else, even the sun going down. While this is the sign of a happy child who has good concentration, a setting sun is often a signal that it's time to go home. Many parents prefer that their children play inside when it's dark outside. Explain why staying out past dark can be unsafe, and then have the children promise that they will be back home at a specific time. Be careful, however, not to instill a fear of the dark.

Why Is It Bad for Us To Sit Right in Front of the TV?

ANSWER Because sitting right in front of the television screen is bad for our eyes. Our eyesight is very precious, and we should take good care of it. And sitting too close is selfish, because it stops other people from enjoying the TV as well.

Playing outdoors whenever we can and getting a good night's rest is much better for us than watching too much TV.

What About When We Are Reading Books?

When reading a book be sure that you're comfortable and that there's plenty of light in the room to read by.

Why Must I Be Nice To My Little Brother?

ANSWER Little brothers and sisters do not understand all the things that you do. They often think that they should have their own way. When you were little you were like that too. Be kind and patient. As your brother grows up he will understand more and more.

No! It's mine! I'm reading it!

Let me borrow it!

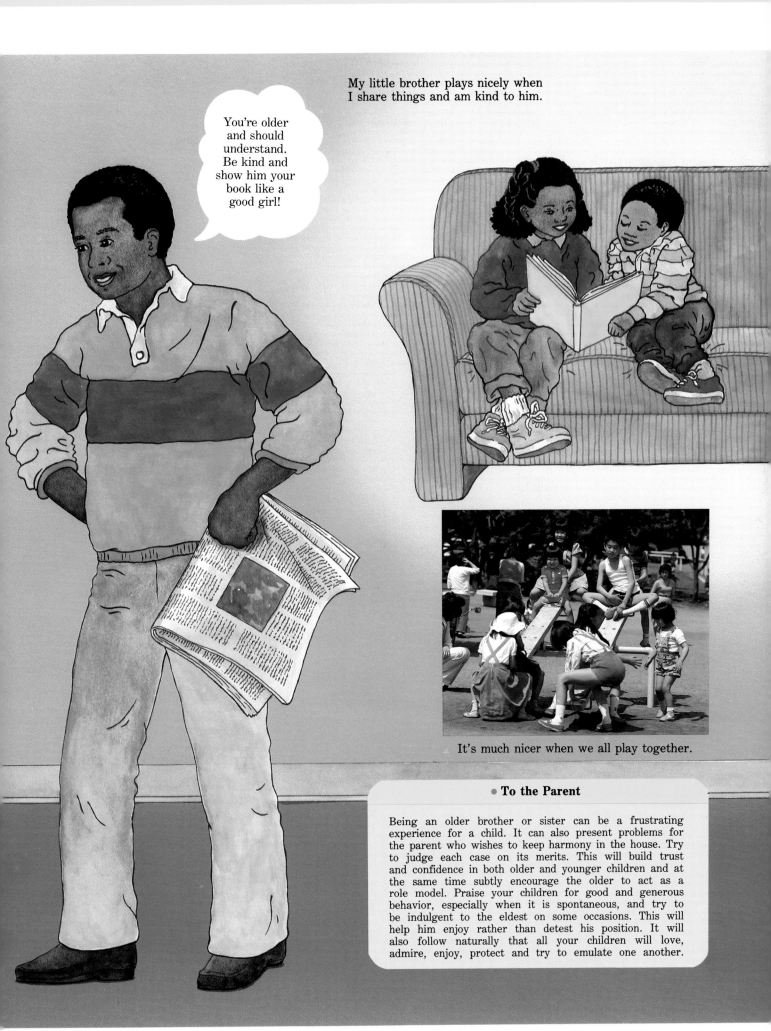

You're older and should understand. Be kind and show him your book like a good girl!

My little brother plays nicely when I share things and am kind to him.

It's much nicer when we all play together.

● **To the Parent**

Being an older brother or sister can be a frustrating experience for a child. It can also present problems for the parent who wishes to keep harmony in the house. Try to judge each case on its merits. This will build trust and confidence in both older and younger children and at the same time subtly encourage the older to act as a role model. Praise your children for good and generous behavior, especially when it is spontaneous, and try to be indulgent to the eldest on some occasions. This will help him enjoy rather than detest his position. It will also follow naturally that all your children will love, admire, enjoy, protect and try to emulate one another.

Why Must We Clean Up?

ANSWER We love playing with the toys and books in our home. These things are important to us. When we put them away we know they will not get lost or broken. That is why we should straighten up when we finish playing.

Ouch!

Now where's the ball gone?

Oh! Put us back into our box!

▲ Put books back on the shelves after you've read them.

▲ Tidying up is fun when everyone lends a hand.

● **To the Parent**

Children get absorbed in one activity after another without ever stopping to clean up. In training them to be tidy it is essential that you provide them with a fixed place to keep their things. Tell them toys and books must be put away when they have finished playing and that things left out may become lost or broken. Encourage your children to develop a sense of affection for their possessions, and that will help them become neat. Teaching by example is the best way, so make sure they see you following the same rules.

Why Do We Take Baths?

ANSWER Imagine what would happen if you didn't take a bath! After playing all day you are dirty and sticky. A bath or shower makes you feel fresh and clean again. When do you like to take your bath?

Oh, rats! What a nuisance! I've got to take a bath!

Now I'm nice and clean, and it feels so good!

● **To the Parent**

It would be sad if your child grew up resenting having to bathe and hating to take a bath, so make bath time a happy time for your child. When children are small and you are still bathing them, make a game out of it, and when they get bigger let them play in the bath with their favorite toys so that bath time becomes fun and they look forward to it. Once this has been achieved it is important to set reasonable limits on the time they are allowed to stay in the bath so they don't catch cold. Once again, teach by example and make them aware that you bathe regularly. Make bathing a habit and fun. The reasons for bathing can be left until they are older.

❓ Why Do We Brush Our Teeth?

ANSWER To brush away the bits of food that get stuck between our teeth and cause toothache and cavities. For healthy teeth brush morning, night and after meals.

What If We Don't Brush Our Teeth?

The bits of food stuck in our teeth start to decay. Germs build up and make our teeth decay. We get toothaches and can't eat properly and have to go to the dentist. Brushing our teeth keeps them strong and white so we can eat a lot and grow up healthy and happy.

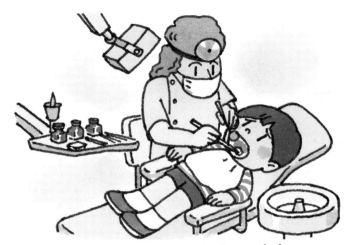

▲ You should be examined by a dentist regularly.

Oh, I hurt! I've got such an awful toothache!

My tooth hurts so much that I can't chew my food.

● **To the Parent**

To avoid serious dental problems in young children parental involvement is essential. Some parents feel that strict supervision of dental hygiene is not so important before a child gets its adult teeth. Nothing could be further from the truth. Unhealthy baby teeth mean that a child's permanent teeth will not develop properly either. Providing a good example and making it fun is the key. Help the children brush their teeth when they are small, and as quickly as possible get them to brush their own, three minutes each morning and evening and after meals. At first check to see that they have done it properly. And limit the sweets that they eat.

Why Do We Have to Go to Bed Even When We're Not Sleepy?

ANSWER Because we're still growing we need lots of sleep to help us grow. Even when we're not sleepy we fall asleep quickly once we're in bed. And we wake up bright and early the next morning. We'd feel tired all day if we went to bed late!

■ If you stay up late

▲ I overslept! And now I'm late for school!

▲ I'm tired and sleepy, and I don't want to play!

Early to bed, early to rise

▲ In bed by 8 o'clock.

▲ Wide awake by seven!

TRY THIS

Children need more sleep than grown-ups because they are still growing. Make it a habit to go to bed before having to be told. If we go to bed early we'll wake up early, happy and ready to face the day. We'll grow up healthy, too!

I went to bed early and got up early. Mother went to bed later than I did, but she was up and making breakfast when I went to brush my teeth. She doesn't look tired, though. So it's true! She doesn't need as much sleep as I do!

● **To the Parent**

A child who is healthy and who has been active during the day should be ready for bed at the appropriate time. It's essential for growing children to get their correct sleep requirement: 11 to 15 hours for those 1 to 3 years and 10 to 12 for those 4 to 9 years old is a good rule. Be firm about bedtime, but try not to give your children the impression that they are missing anything. If you keep the television and other noise to a minimum when you put them to bed they will soon be sound asleep. And they will wake up eager to face another new day.

Why Do We Try to Blow Out All Our Birthday Candles at Once?

ANSWER We put candles on a birthday cake to make it special. There are the same number of candles as our age. Make a wish and blow out the candles. If you can blow them all out at once your wish may come true. What do you like to wish for?

■ How many candles on a birthday cake?

A birthday cake usually has the same number of candles as your age, but sometimes there is one extra for good luck. As you get older you will need more air to blow them all out in one breath.

❓ How Does a Key Unlock a Door?

ANSWER A lock has many tiny metal bolts inside it. These bolts hold the door closed. To open it the bolts must be pushed into a perfect position. If we put in the right key the bolts move, and the door will open.

101

■ How a lock works

There are many kinds of locks in use, but the most common kind is perhaps the pin tumbler lock shown below. When no key is inserted, the springs press against the drivers and push the pins into the plug, preventing it from turning. When the right key is inserted it presses the drivers into the cylinder, while the pins come into line but remain in the plug. When the key is turned, the plug turns inside the cylinder and releases a bolt that kept the lock shut. This type of lock may have 3 to 10 of the bolts, which are called pin tumblers, depending on how much security the lock must provide. Each key must be cut so that it will make the pins align precisely with the shear line.

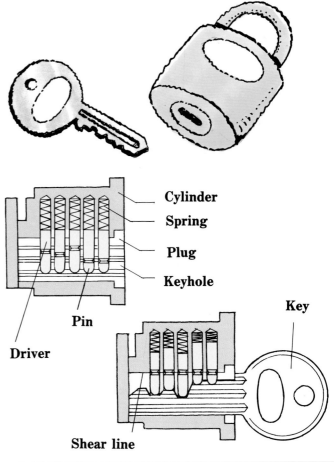

Cylinder

Spring

Plug

Keyhole

Key

Pin

Driver

Shear line

● **To the Parent**

Locks have been used since the beginning of recorded history to help people protect valuable property from intruders and thieves. The oldest known lock that functioned mechanically was used in Egypt about 2000 B. C. That one worked in a way similar to that of the pin tumbler lock illustrated above. It was much simpler, of course, and was made of wood, but it served its purpose. When metal locks were developed, some of the earlier ones offered little protection except by the shape of the keyhole. If a key could pass through that, it could operate the lock. Later locksmiths developed locks with hidden keyholes. The combination lock was in use by the late 16th Century. In this lock, slots in disks matched numbers on the dial. When these lined up evenly the bolt could be withdrawn. These led to the giant bank vaults of today. The Yale lock so popular now was patented in 1861 by an American, Linus Yale.

 Why Do We Have Money?

ANSWER A long time ago people did not use money. They traded for the things they needed. But this was not always easy to do. And different things are not always worth the same amount. So people printed money as a simple and easy way to buy and sell things.

Every country prints its own money. Here you see some money from different nations. Look at some bills from your country. How are they like the money you see here? How are they different?

What Money Can Buy

▲ A pair of shoes

▲ Notebooks and pencils

▲ A pretty dress

▲ Good food

Why Do So Many People Put Their Money in Banks?

ANSWER Sometimes we earn more money than we need. When that happens many people put the extra money in a bank. Your money can be lost or stolen if it is kept at home. In a bank it is much safer. And banks pay people extra money called interest, so that your money will grow in value in the bank.

Where Does Our Money Go?

Most banks have a giant steel safe called a vault. The lock on a vault opens only at certain times for added safety.

Banks Keep Other Things Too

Many banks have safe-deposit boxes for people to rent. The customers keep many different things in these boxes. Some put their important papers in them, and others keep jewelry and other valuable items there. What would you put in one?

Many banks have giant vaults where they keep their valuable things when the bank is closed.

● **To the Parent**

In our complex modern world banks have become a basic part of most people's lives. In addition to safeguarding money and paying interest on invested assets, most banks provide people with a simplified system of paying bills through the use of checks and provide loans for people who are in need of cash. If your child does not already have one you might want to consider opening a savings account in his or her name. It would take only a modest investment to help them learn the value of money and the importance of saving.

❓ How Does a Light Bulb Make Light?

ANSWER Most bulbs, like the one shown below, have a very thin metal wire in them. Electricity passes through the wire, making it so hot that it glows white, and that makes light. This bulb gets very hot and may burn you if you touch it. Other bulbs make light because the electricity is mixed with gases and chemicals, and that also makes light.

■ A common light bulb

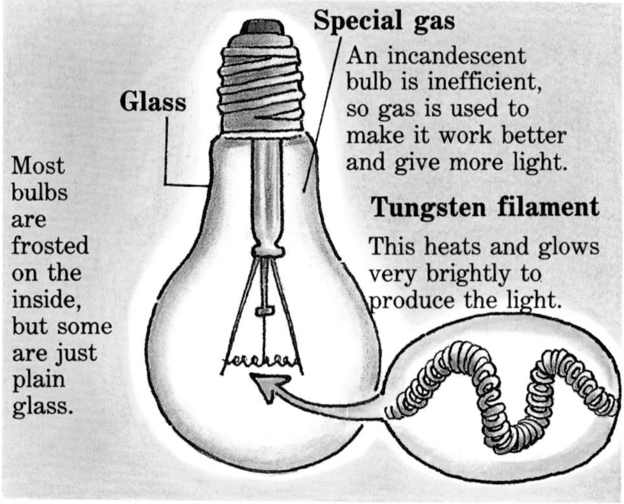

Glass

Most bulbs are frosted on the inside, but some are just plain glass.

Special gas

An incandescent bulb is inefficient, so gas is used to make it work better and give more light.

Tungsten filament

This heats and glows very brightly to produce the light.

Different Bulbs

▲ Here are five bulbs. Which ones have you seen before?

▲ Well-lighted places attract customers.

▲ The city is pretty when all the lights are turned on.

● **To the Parent**

The top drawing shows two incandescent bulbs, a photoflood and two fluorescent bulbs. The incandescent bulb on page 60 has an extremely fine tungsten filament. Mercury vapor in fluorescent lamps excites a phosphor coating inside the bulb and causes the phosphor to emit light. These lights are very popular in offices.

Why Do We See Ourselves When We Look Into a Mirror?

ANSWER On the back of the glass of a mirror is a very thin coat of silver or aluminum. We say that it is silvered even when the coating is made of aluminum. Any glass that is silvered will reflect light and make images of whatever is in front of it. That is very handy when you need to wash your face or comb your hair. Watching yourself in the mirror makes it real easy!

MINI-DATA

Almost every boy and girl has looked into a pool of water and seen a reflection of his or her face. You might call that pool the world's first mirror, for it is likely that a still pool of water was the first thing that allowed people to look at their own faces. If there are ripples on the water the picture is not very good, is it? For the same reason, glass that is not truly smooth does not make a really good mirror.

Tricky Mirrors

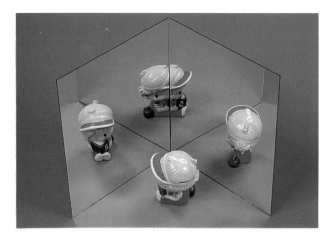

Some mirrors sure do funny things!

● **To the Parent**

Fun-house mirrors distort images because their surfaces curve differently. Concave surfaces will magnify an image. Convex ones reduce it. Others stretch it. At top two mirrors make three images. Glass mirrors were in use by the 16th Century, and silver coating began in 1840. But silver tarnished easily, so today most glass mirrors use aluminum. Backed glass mirrors cannot be used in astronomical telescopes because the front of the glass itself gives off a faint reflection in addition to the strong one produced by its silvered back. Mirrors for those are a mix of aluminum and Pyrex glass.

Why Do Men Wear Ties to Work?

ANSWER People must wear the right clothes for their jobs. Many women and men must dress neatly. The men often wear sports jackets and ties.

■ Places where ties are worn

The office. People who work in offices must dress neatly. Suits and ties are a kind of uniform that many men wear. You can see in the picture above that some women wear business suits made for them.

At parties. When men and women go to parties they often wear their nicest clothes. At fancy parties men wear a special coat called a tuxedo. When dressed in a tuxedo, a man always wears a bow tie.

■ How men's ties got their start

There sure were a lot of different ties before they looked like the ones we have today!

For many centuries men have worn things around their necks. About 600 years ago men wore a special coat called a doublet. This tight-fitting coat had a large ruffled collar. More than 300 years ago Englishmen wore a kind of bow around their necks. At the same time some European soldiers wore uniforms that included a bright piece of cloth tied at the neck. When they served the king of France their uniforms caught the fancy of Frenchmen. Soon it became the fashion in Paris, France, to tie cloth in this way. Since that time neckties have continued to change along with people's taste in clothing. The drawings above show you how ties have changed style over the last 200 years.

● **To the Parent**

While people all over the world today express a liking for more casual wear the necktie has for hundreds of years been considered the mark of a well-dressed man. They have evolved from the fancy wrap-around bow of 1795 seen at the upper left in the drawing to the four-in-hand (second from right, bottom row) that men wear to this day. Even this style changes almost yearly as fashion designers develop new styles to make old ties out of date and to help sell more new ties.

How Do Some Doors Open and Close by Themselves?

ANSWER They work by hidden switches and open when the switch is pressed. Most close by themselves after a short while. Many slide from side to side, but some open in and out. All work by electricity and can hit you and hurt you if you stand in them or play too close to them.

How Do They Work?

Automatic doors have different kinds of switches. Some work when a beam of light is broken by someone crossing it. People often call this an electric eye. Many switches are covered by mats in front of the door. Other doors have a plate which contains a switch that you push to open the door.
A door that opens in and out is dangerous. If you are standing in front of it and it is opened by someone else, you could be injured quite badly.

▲ The switch for this one is under the doormat.

▲ The electric eye in the ceiling works this door.

▶ This touch switch is low enough for a small boy.

❓ Why Do I Have to Get a Haircut Even if It Itches?

ANSWER Partly for looks and partly because it is easier to keep your hair clean when it is shorter. The itching will go away when the loose hairs that get down your neck have been washed off.

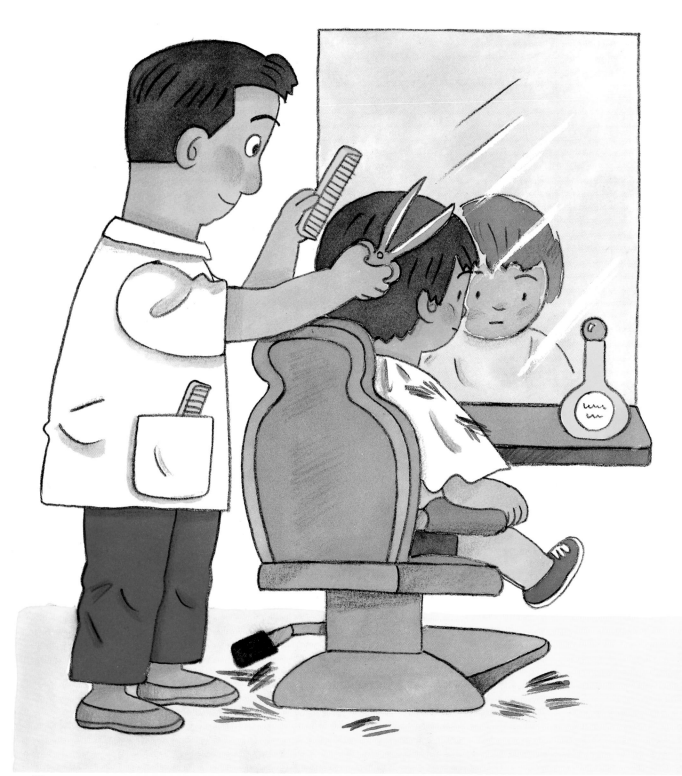

Long ago when people lived in caves and used clubs for hunting, their hair got pretty long. Pretty dirty too. They did not have the right tools to cut hair. Today there are barbershops where you can get a haircut like the boy below. Then you should always keep it neat and clean.

● To the Parent

Since antiquity people have oiled their hair, dyed it, curled it and done any number of other things to enhance its appearance. Primitive tribes plastered their hair with clay, and some of them still do. In ancient Greece and Rome the barbershop was not just a place for cutting hair but a forum for exchanging gossip, and to this day the reputation survives. At one time, when it was considered beneficial to the health, barbers did bloodletting. The red on the pole that identifies their shops is a symbol of the bloody bandages once associated with them.

Why Does Water Run Out of a Faucet?

ANSWER The water is already in the pipe. There are two parts that fit together and do not let water out as long as the handle is closed. If you turn the handle the two parts separate and leave a hole that the water can pass through. If you look at the diagram below you can see how water goes from the faucet into the sink.

How a faucet works

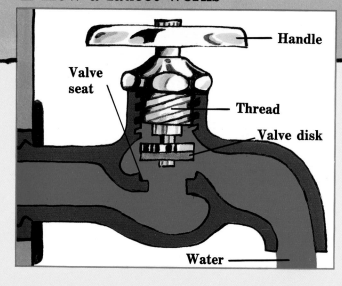

Handle

Valve seat

Thread

Valve disk

Water

When the handle is turned to the right the thread drives the valve disk down to fit tightly into the valve seat, and that stops the flow of water. In this diagram the valve disk is not seated in the valve seat, so the water flows out of the spout.

Fun With Water

When the weather is very hot it is fun to sprinkle the lawn or water the flowers with the garden hose. There is a nozzle on the end of the hose, and even after you open the faucet the water will not come out until you also open the nozzle. Many boys and girls like to wet one another with the garden hose, and it is a nice game if you are dressed properly for it, but you should not play water games when you are wearing your nice clothes. After you finish playing outside you can enjoy a nice bath with lots and lots of bubbles and some of your favorite toys.

● **To the Parent**

Most common faucets around the home and even those used in most industries are of the type illustrated on page 70. When the screw-type plug, or valve disk, is fully seated no water can pass unless the valve is faulty. If there is a leak the valve should be fitted with a new gasket. That is the job of a plumber, but some people like to do it themselves. Before a gasket is changed the water should be shut off at its source to prevent flooding when the faucet mechanism is taken apart.

Why Do the Lights Go Off When I Push the Switch?

ANSWER Bulbs light because they are receiving electricity that comes into our houses from outside. There are several ways to cut off the current, and switches are one of them. If you push the switch and stop the electricity the light goes out, and the room goes dark.

Lines and switches

You can see electric lines for some switches, but sometimes they are in the wall behind the switch.

This ceiling light has no switch attached. The switch for it is on the wall, usually near a door.

Power lines like these carry the electricity that makes lights and appliances in your home work.

Why Do People Working on Buildings Wear Those Funny Hats?

ANSWER On a construction site heavy things sometimes fall or are dropped. If they fell on someone's head it would hurt, so hard hats are usually worn for protection.

The danger is usually up above.

On many jobs workers also wear shoes with a steel cap over the toes and the front part of the foot to protect them. Some of them have steel in the sole so that if the wearer steps on a nail it won't hurt. There are also special goggles to protect the eyes, and special gloves, depending on the type of work that is being done.

It's a good thing I'm wearing a hard hat!

● **To the Parent**

There are many types of safety equipment besides that named here. The hard hat that is worn by so many workers, and not only on construction jobs, is made more effective because its inner suspension spreads the shock of a falling object over a wider area of the head. These hats have generally followed the shape of a military helmet. They were once made of metal, but today most of them are made of an extremely hard plastic. Other safety gear includes the welder's helmet, which shields the eyes not only from flying sparks but also from the fiery bright flame of the torch. One special cap reduces the chance that a worker's hair might be caught by the moving parts of a machine or be pulled into the machine by static electricity.

❓ Why Do Police Wear Uniforms?

ANSWER Police are there to protect people. They wear uniforms so you can easily see who they are. The uniforms are different for each country and sometimes also for different jobs—police station superintendents or traffic police, for example.

Police are also there to help prevent crime. If a person about to commit a crime sees a police officer in uniform it may stop him or her from doing it.

Police help you. I like them!

● **To the Parent**

Most authorities agree that police presence is the principal deterrent to crime, whether it is a foot patrol or police in cars. The personality of the person in uniform is an important factor. If children know that the police are their friends they will be much more apt to turn to them for help if it is ever needed. Teach your children that they should not be awed by the police but should regard them as friends who can help them.

What Kind of People Need to Wear Uniforms?

ANSWER The police are not the only people who need to wear uniforms. Many other people need to be easily recognized. Still others wear a uniform because it is suitable clothing for the job they do. That's why soldiers, nurses, athletes and even schoolchildren can be seen in various kinds of uniforms.

Gee, there sure are a lot of uniforms. There must be one for every job!

▲ Police   ▲ Soldier   ▲ Chef   ▲ Nurse   ▲ Basketball player

■ Some people wear uniforms for safety

Some jobs are dangerous. So people wear special clothing to protect them. A race driver needs protection against crashes, and a football player needs protection because the game is very rough.

▲ Welder

▲ Firefighter

▲ Astronaut

■ Children wear uniforms too

Some children wear uniforms when they go to school. Some wear them when they play on an athletic team. Sometimes special clubs have uniforms for members. Do you wear a uniform?

▲ Students

▲ Soccer players

● **To the Parent**

The wearing of uniforms for protection or identification is common in most countries around the world. The uniform varies according to the country, and its form is affected by climate, local custom and available fabric. With your help your children will probably be able to recall a time when they were required to wear a uniform. It might have been when they marched with the school band, or perhaps when one of them was a star on the school baseball team.

What's Happening Here?

■ Archery on horseback

This is a festival they hold in Japan. Archers mounted on speeding horses and dressed in costumes of ancient times shoot arrows at a colorful target. They compete to see who can shoot an arrow closest to the bull's-eye at the center of the target. It's not at all easy! The archer needs both hands to shoot his arrow, and so all he has are his knees to steer his galloping horse.

■ Firemen's acrobatics

Firemen's acrobatics, old and new, form a traditional part of the New Year's celebrations in Japan. Above, firemen perform with great skill at the top of bamboo ladders. On the right a uniformed fireman stands by two modern fire engines, their ladders extended.

Growing-Up Album

Record of Family Firsts

The simple accomplishments of a child
are an important part of everyday life.
Use these pages to create a book of
memories. Chances may be that your child
is already past these important "firsts."
Share your recollections with your child
and have him or her write down the
different things each of you remember.

■ **My first words**

■ **The first time I washed my face by myself was...**

_____

_____

_____

_____

■ **The first time I dressed myself all on my own was...**

_____

_____

_____

_____

■ **The first time I combed my hair by myself was...**

_____

_____

_____

_____

■ **The first time I brushed my own teeth was...**

_____

_____

_____

_____

■ **The first time I went to the dentist was...**

_____

_____

_____

_____

Record of Things I Enjoyed

■ New Year

_____

_____

_____

_____

_____

■ My birthday

_____

_____

_____

_____

_____

■ School started

_____

_____

_____

_____

_____

■ Important questions

_____

_____

_____

_____

_____

_____

_____

■ **My pets**

_____
_____
_____
_____

■ **My friends**

_____
_____
_____
_____

■ **School was out**

_____
_____
_____
_____

■ **Vacations**

_____
_____
_____
_____

_____
_____
_____
_____
_____
_____
_____
_____
_____

What Is Everybody Doing?

■ Look at this picture carefully

All of the animals on the right can also be found in the picture above. Some are there more than once. How many can you find? Use the clues with the animals to make sure that you have found the right picture.

I'm buying vegetables.

I brush every day.

I'm washing u

It's TV time.

I'm going for a ride.

It's my turn to slide.

A Child's First Library of Learning

Everyday Life

Time-Life Books is a division of Time Life Inc.,
a wholly owned subsidiary of
The Time Inc. Book Company
Time-Life Books, Alexandria, Virginia
Children's Publishing

Publisher:	Robert H. Smith
Managing Editor:	Neil Kagan
Associate Editors:	Jean Burke Crawford
	Patricia Daniels
Marketing Director:	Ruth P. Stevens
Promotion Director:	Kathleen B. Tresnak
Associate Promotion Director:	Jane B. Welihozkiy
Production Manager:	Prudence G. Harris
Editorial Consultants:	Jacqueline A. Ball
	Andrew Gutelle
	Sara Mark

Editorial Supervision by:
International Editorial Services Inc.
Tokyo, Japan

Editor:	C. E. Berry
Associate Editor:	Winston S. Priest
Translation:	Joseph Hlebica
	Bryan Harrell
Writer:	Pauline Bush
Editorial Staff:	Christine Alaimo
	Nobuko Abe

Cover:	Roger Foley

Library of Congress Cataloging in Publication Data
Everyday life.
    (A Child's first library of learning)
    Summary: Answers questions about manners, behavior, responsibility, hygiene, and everyday life in the United States. An activities section is included.
    ISBN 0-8094-4865-3   ISBN 0-8094-4866-1 (lib. bdg.)
    1. United States—Social life and customs—1971-
    —Miscellanea—Juvenile literature. 2. Children—United States—Life skills guides—Juvenile literature. 3. Self-reliance in children—Miscellanea—Juvenile literature. 4. Children's questions and answers.
[1. United States—Social life and customs—1971-
    —Miscellanea. 2. Conduct of life—Miscellanea. 3. Questions and answers]
I. Time-Life Books.   II. Series.
E169.04.E85 1990   649'.124   89-20406
© 1989 Time-Life Books Inc.
© 1988 Gakken Co. Ltd.

Third printing 1992. Printed in U.S.A.
Published simultaneously in Canada.

TIME-LIFE is a trademark of Time Warner Inc. U.S.A.